EXPLORE NATURAL RESOURCES!

Anita Yasuda

Illustrated by Jennifer K. Keller

Newest titles in the **Explore Your World!** Series

Nomad Press
A division of Nomad Communications
10 9 8 7 6 5 4 3 2 1

This book was manufactured by McNaughton & Gunn, Inc., Saline, MI USA.
May 2014, Job #500901
ISBN: 978-1-61930-223-5

Illustrations by Jennifer K. Keller
Educational Consultant, Marla Conn

Questions regarding the ordering of this book should be addressed to
Nomad Press
2456 Christian St.
White River Junction, VT 05001
www.nomadpress.net

Nomad Press is committed to preserving ancient
forests and natural resources.

We elected to print *Explore Natural Resources! With 25 Great Projects*
on paper containing 100% post consumer waste.

CONTENTS

LET'S EXPLORE NATURAL RESOURCES!

Do you like to play soccer or go swimming? Kicking a soccer ball across a field, scrambling up a huge pile of rocks, and jumping into your favorite swimming hole are all fun activities. They're also activities that make use of the earth's **natural resources**. But what are natural resources? Where can you find them? Why can't you live without them? And why should you protect them?

WORDS TO KNOW

natural resource: something from nature that people can use in some way, such as water, stone, and wood.

1

WORDS TO KNOW

soil: the top layer of the earth, in which plants grow.

mineral: something found in nature that is not an animal or plant, such as gold, salt, or copper.

energy: the ability to do work.

environmentalist: a person who works to keep the earth healthy.

preserve: to keep safe from injury, harm, or destruction.

conserve: to avoid wasteful use of something.

recycle: to use something again.

In this book you'll explore a few of the earth's fascinating natural resources, including air, water, **soil**, and **minerals**. Without these resources, many of the activities you enjoy wouldn't be possible. In fact, life wouldn't be possible!

You will discover that natural resources are used as building materials, sources of **energy**, and for creating medicine. *Explore Natural Resources!* will answer many of your questions and introduce you to **environmentalists** such as Theodore Roosevelt and John Muir along the way. Learning about natural resources also means discovering how you can make choices to **preserve**, **conserve**, and protect them.

JUST FOR LAUGHS

WHY DID THE BOY KNOCK OVER A GLASS OF WATER?

He wanted to see the waterfall!

You'll discover the world of natural resources by working on lots of fun experiments and activities. You'll come across silly jokes and interesting facts too. By the end of this book you'll be able to design a wind-powered car, make a Leonardo da Vinci–inspired solar catcher, build a composter, and Reduce, Reuse, and **Recycle**.

What are you waiting for? It's time to splash in the water and dig in the soil. Put on your shoes, grab your backpack, and get ready to *Explore Natural Resources!* Treat them with care!

WHAT IS A NATURAL RESOURCE?

The earth is an incredible planet that provides you with all the natural resources you need. People can't create natural resources—they come from nature.

How many natural resources do you think there are? Would you say more than 100? In fact, there are thousands of natural resources on and in the earth. They include the sun shining overhead, the air you breathe, and the soil under your feet.

WORDS TO KNOW

raw material: a natural resource used to make something.

goods: things to use or sell.

Many times we use natural resources and don't even realize it. This is because we use them as building blocks, called **raw materials**, to make everyday objects. You might have one of these objects in your back pocket right now, such as a piece of paper.

THEN & NOW

Early settlers used wooden containers, pails, or cloth bags to transport **goods** to their homes. They used these containers over and over again.

The average American family uses 1,500 plastic shopping bags per year. Less than 1 percent are recycled. That's only 15 out of 1,500 bags.

3

Even the clothes you wear are made from natural resources. Your jeans are made of cotton. Cotton plants need soil, sun, and water to grow. If your pants have a metal button, it came from mineral **deposits** such as copper buried deep in the earth. The dye came from **petroleum**. A **factory** used machines that require energy to clean and sew the final product. And these are just a few of the natural resources that went into making that one pair of jeans!

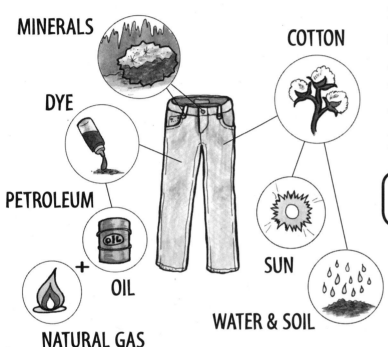

MINERALS

DYE

PETROLEUM

OIL

NATURAL GAS

COTTON

SUN

WATER & SOIL

USING NATURAL RESOURCES

WORDS TO KNOW

deposit: a layer of something, such as sand or salt.

petroleum: a thick, dark liquid that occurs naturally beneath the surface of the earth. It can be separated into many products, including gasoline and other fuels.

factory: a place where goods are made.

Throughout human history, people have been discovering more uses for natural resources. Roughly 3 million years ago, people were hunters and gatherers who had to move often in search of food. They lived simply, using only about 6 pounds (3 kilograms) of natural resources a day. That's about the weight of a large pizza with toppings!

About 10,000 **BCE**, in the **Middle East** and later in other areas of the globe, people began making tools from stone. Called the Stone Age, this was the time people learned to grow **crops**. They also learned to use animals—not just for food and clothing, but also for work and transportation. Later, they learned to melt and mix metals to create tools and weapons.

WORDS TO KNOW

BCE: put after a date, BCE stands for Before Common Era and counts years down to zero. CE stands for Common Era and counts years up from zero. The year this book was published is 2014 CE.

Middle East: the countries of Southwest Asia and North Africa, from Libya in the west to Afghanistan in the east.

crops: plants grown for food and other uses.

society: an organized **community** of people.

community: a group of people who live in the same area.

industrial society: a society that relies on machines to make goods.

People living in these farming **societies** used around 24 pounds (11 kilograms) of natural resources each day. Think of that as three gallons of milk. That's still not a lot, but it's more than the hunters and gatherers used.

Practically everything we do requires natural resources—and lots of them! Today, we live in **industrial societies**. Each person in industrial societies uses an average of 97 pounds (44 kilograms) of natural resources a day. How much does this add up to? The weight of all the natural resources taken from the earth every day is equivalent to 112 Empire State buildings. Now that's a lot!

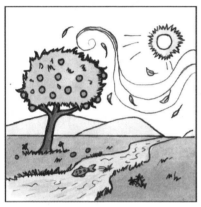

Have you heard that more isn't always better? That's certainly true of how we use our natural resources. Some scientists worry that the earth cannot keep up with how quickly people are using its resources.

Some natural resources are **renewable**. Sunlight, air, soil, fresh water, and plants are examples of renewable resources. We use them daily, but if we are very careful with them they shouldn't run out. These resources can replace themselves.

But other natural resources are **nonrenewable**, such as **fossil fuels**. Oil and coal are fossil fuels. We use them all the time to keep our homes warm and our cars running. But it takes millions of years for these resources to form again. This means that once we use them, they're gone and cannot be replaced.

WORDS TO KNOW

renewable: a resource that nature can replace.

nonrenewable: something you can run out of, such as oil that will run out one day.

fossil fuels: fuels made from the remains of ancient plants and animals, including coal, oil, petroleum, and natural gas.

STRESSED OUT

Unfortunately, we are stressing the earth as people continue to use more and more resources. The **demand** for natural resources is increasing. The way the resources are taken from the earth and the **waste** produced by using them have created problems.

Some of these problems include **polluted** soil, air, and water, as well as destroyed **ecosystems**. Ecosystems are areas called **habitats**, where plants, animals, and other **organisms** live. Plants, animals and, yes, even humans, depend on habitats for survival.

WORDS TO KNOW

demand: how much of something people want.

waste: unwanted material that can harm the environment.

pollute: to make dirty or unclean with chemicals or other waste.

ecosystem: a community of living and nonliving things and their environment. Living things are plants, animals, and insects. Nonliving things are soil, rocks, and water.

habitat: an area that a plant or animal calls home.

organism: any living thing.

ENERGETIC FLOORS

Floor tiles are more than just decoration. A company called Pavegan Systems has created tiles that actually collect energy when people walk over them. When a person walks on these special tiles, the energy from their footsteps is converted into electricity! The tiles have been used in schools, malls, and subways to power lights, signs, and even Wi-Fi hotspots.

When a habitat is damaged or destroyed, the plants and animals that live there are **displaced** or become **extinct**. Earth loses some of its **biodiversity**. Imagine sitting in a park and not seeing plants, trees, or birds. It's not a pretty picture, is it?

WORDS TO KNOW

displace: to force people or animals to move from their home.

extinct: when a group of plants or animals dies out and there are no more left in the world.

biodiversity: the different plants, animals, and other living things in an area.

species: a group of plants or animals that are related and look the same.

Conservation International estimates that a **species** goes extinct every 20 minutes. Many of these species go extinct because their habitats have been destroyed.

You may not think that extinction affects your life, but it does. For example, more than half of the medicines available today use chemicals found in plants. What medicines are still to be discovered? If a plant becomes extinct, its special chemicals that might give us new medicines are gone, too.

DID YOU KNOW?

Out of every five animal and plant species, one is threatened by extinction. There are many reasons for extinction, including disease and pollution. Some experts believe that as many as 150 to 200 species of plants, insects, birds, and mammals become extinct every 24 hours. It is happening the fastest in Southeast Asia, where people are clearing away a lot of forest for farmland.

CONSERVATION

Trees, water, air, and land are all part of a giant team called the **environment**. And guess what? You're part of this team too! When one member or resource is harmed, it causes a **chain reaction**. Everything on the earth is connected. So what can you do? Take action!

As you already know, our planet is special. It can't be replaced, and neither can many of the resources you are going to read about. So your actions are really important. In this book you are going to learn creative ways to keep the earth healthy— by conserving natural resources through reducing, reusing, and recycling.

WORDS TO KNOW

environment: everything in nature, living and nonliving, including animals, plants, rocks, soil, and water.

chain reaction: when things are so connected that a change to one causes a change in the others.

You might feel that one person can't make a difference, but that isn't true. Your actions can impact your family, friends, and even your community.

Learning to make good decisions each time you buy or get rid of products makes the world greener. This doesn't mean painting the world green. Green represents nature. Making the world greener means taking good care of the earth. When you turn the last page of this book, you may look at the world around you a little differently. And just maybe, your new favorite color will be green!

EARTH DAY

April 22 is Earth Day. It was founded in 1970 by Gaylord Nelson, a senator from Wisconsin. He thought people should start taking better care of the environment. Today, Earth Day is celebrated all over the world with people picking up trash on beaches, along roads, and on school playgrounds. It is a day spent planting trees and gardens, too.

WHO LIVES IN YOUR NEIGHBORHOOD?

Invite an adult or friend to discover the animals and plants that call your community home. Remember, some animals and plants only appear in certain seasons. **NOTE: This activity requires going online. Ask an adult to supervise while you are on the Internet.**

1 Write the following headings on your paper: "birds," "reptiles," "mammals," "trees," and "plants." Think about what fits into each heading.

2 Draw a picture from each category or cut out examples from magazines.

3 Place your paper on a clipboard and take it along on your hike. Don't forget a pencil to record your observations.

4 As you walk, listen and look for creatures, plants, and trees on your list. Take photos if you brought your camera or smart phone.

5 After your hike, print your photos and add these images to your list. Or go online with the permission of an adult and find photos of plants and animals to print out.

SUPPLIES

- paper and pencil
- magazines
- scissors
- glue
- clipboard
- camera or phone

THINGS TO THINK ABOUT: Did you see and hear a lot of different animal and birds? How would the season lead you to see more or less of these creatures? Where could you go to see more?

MAP YOUR STATE'S NATURAL RESOURCES

Make a three-dimensional map to give you an understanding of the natural resources in your state. This map will include natural resources found in your state, such as fish or forests, but not products made by them. **NOTE: This activity requires going online. Ask an adult to supervise while you are on the Internet.**

1 Place the salt and flour in a bowl. Add the cream of tartar and enough water to make the dough thick.

2 Start your map by placing the dough on the cardboard and pressing it into a large rectangle.

3 See **worldatlas.com** or **50states.com** for outline maps of your state. Print and cut out a state map.

4 Place the paper map over the salt dough and trim off the excess dough with a plastic knife.

SUPPLIES

- bowl and spoon
- 2 cups salt (475 milliliters)
- 2 cups flour (475 milliliters)
- 2 tablespoons cream of tartar (30 milliliters)
- water
- cardboard, 15 by 20 inches (38 by 50 centimeters)
- Internet
- scissors
- plastic knife
- paint
- paintbrush
- paper and pencil
- tape or glue
- toothpicks

5 Research which natural resources are used in your state. Try **education.nationalgeographic.com** or **kids.britannica.com** to learn more about resources in North America.

6 Use leftover dough to make small models of the natural resources found in your state, such as water, timber, cattle, or minerals.

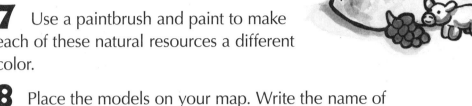

7 Use a paintbrush and paint to make each of these natural resources a different color.

8 Place the models on your map. Write the name of each resource on a piece of paper and tape it to a toothpick. Push the toothpicks into the correct region on your map.

9 Let your map dry.

JUST FOR LAUGHS

WHY DON'T THE SUN AND THE WIND PLAY WITH PLASTIC?

Because it isn't natural!

AMAZING AIR

WORDS TO KNOW

gas: a substance that can fill up a container, such as air filling your lungs. A gas does not have a definite shape—it spreads out to fill the space it's in.

carbon dioxide: the gas that's produced as a waste product by your body.

water vapor: water as a gas, such as steam, mist, or fog.

Air is like an invisible superhero. It doesn't leap tall buildings, but the power of air surrounds us. So how do we know air is really there? We can see and feel what it does! Place your hand on your chest and take a few deep breaths. Did you feel your chest moving in and out? That was air filling your lungs. In one day you breathe in about 3,000 gallons (11,356 liters) of air.

But what is air exactly? Air is a mixture of **gases**, including nitrogen, oxygen, and **carbon dioxide**. Oxygen is what you breathe in. Carbon dioxide is what you breathe out. Air also contains **water vapor** and dust.

LIVING THINGS AND OXYGEN

Almost all living things on the earth need oxygen. But there are some living things that don't need oxygen to survive. These are called **anaerobic** organisms. They live in places that don't have very much oxygen, such as the bottom of muddy ponds.

Where does oxygen come from? Plants make it! Plants have tiny **pores** on their leaves that they use to "breathe." These pores are called stomata. The stomata allow gases to go in and out of the plant. During **photosynthesis**, plants turn carbon dioxide and water into sugar and oxygen. Photosynthesis gives us the oxygen we need. That's why plants are so important.

WORDS TO KNOW

anaerobic: living without oxygen.

pore: a tiny opening.

photosynthesis: the process a plant goes through to make its own food. The plant uses water and carbon dioxide in the presence of sunlight to make oxygen and sugar.

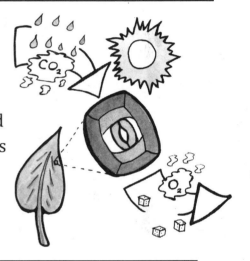

WHO WAS JOSEPH PRIESTLEY?

What is air? In 1773, British scientist Joseph Priestley conducted experiments that led him to discover oxygen. When Priestley placed a large glass jar over a lit candle, the flame went out. He placed a plant under the jar with the candle to see if the plant released something that would make the candle light. He waited several days before trying to relight the candle. It worked! The plant gave off the oxygen the candle needed.

THE ATMOSPHERE

Imagine living somewhere that's burning hot during the day and freezing cold at night. You would have to trade in your sweatshirt and jeans for an astronaut suit. This place isn't in some galaxy far, far away. It's the earth without an **atmosphere**.

Atmosphere is the word used to describe the gases that surround the earth, including the air we breathe. The atmosphere isn't made only of air. It is also made of water, wind, and clouds.

WORDS TO KNOW

atmosphere: the gases surrounding the earth or another planet.

absorb: to soak up a liquid or take in energy, heat, light, or sound.

The atmosphere has many important jobs. One big job is to **absorb** heat from the sun. This keeps temperatures on the earth from being too hot or too cold. It also protects you from the sun's dangerous rays.

The atmosphere wraps around your home and the entire planet. It even extends way up into space. The atmosphere is divided into layers with very long names: troposphere, stratosphere, mesosphere, thermosphere, and exosphere. The layers closer to the earth are the thickest. The layers farther away are thinner and eventually become part of space.

JUST FOR LAUGHS

WHY DID THE RESTAURANT ON THE MOON CLOSE?

It had great food, but no atmosphere!

The troposphere is the layer closest to the earth. Its thickness depends on where you are. For example, over the **equator** the troposphere is 11 miles (18 kilometers) thick. You could also call this the weather layer. It is in the troposphere that air forms clouds and rain falls.

WORDS TO KNOW

equator: an invisible line circling the globe halfway between the North and South poles.

ozone layer: the layer in the stratosphere that absorbs most of the sun's radiation.

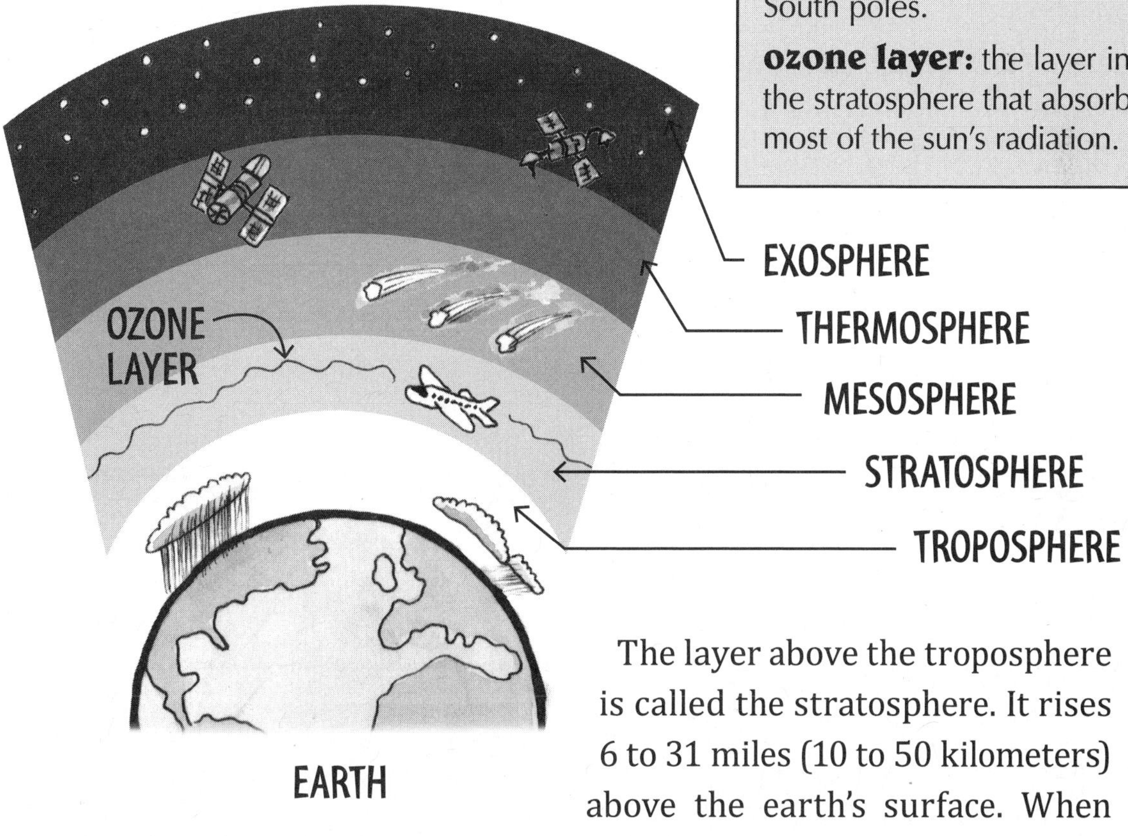

OZONE LAYER

EARTH

EXOSPHERE

THERMOSPHERE

MESOSPHERE

STRATOSPHERE

TROPOSPHERE

The layer above the troposphere is called the stratosphere. It rises 6 to 31 miles (10 to 50 kilometers) above the earth's surface. When you see an airplane in the sky, it's flying in the lower region of the stratosphere. This layer usually has no clouds. It's where the **ozone layer** is located.

The mesosphere stretches 31 to 50 miles (50 to 80 kilometers) above the surface of the earth. It has the coldest temperatures in the atmosphere. Have you ever seen a shooting star? That was a meteor burning up in the mesosphere. Most meteors burn up in this layer.

The thermosphere is the thickest layer of the atmosphere. Only light gases such as oxygen and helium are found here. It reaches 429 miles (690 kilometers) above the surface of the earth. The International Space Station, **communication satellites**, and the Hubble Space Telescope **orbit** the earth in the thermosphere. Have you ever seen the Northern or Southern lights? These electrical displays are created in this layer.

The exosphere is the upper limit of the earth's atmosphere. It extends from the thermosphere up to 6,200 miles (10,000 kilometers) above the earth. The air in the exosphere becomes thinner and thinner until it eventually merges with space.

WORDS TO KNOW

communication satellite: an object placed in orbit around the earth to relay television, radio, and telephone signals.

orbit: the path of an object circling another object in space.

DID YOU KNOW?

Tropical rainforests are nicknamed the "lungs of the world." They produce about 20 percent of the world's oxygen. Rainforests are also home to half the world's plant and animal species. It is thought that 25 percent of all medicines are made from plants that grow in the rainforest!

AIR POLLUTION

It feels great to breathe in fresh air, but polluted air can make you cough. It can also damage your lungs and make you sick. This is because tiny **pollutants** can get stuck in your lungs.

There are two kinds of pollutants. Natural air pollutants are caused by wildfires, dust storms, or volcano blasts. Natural disasters create smoke and dust pollution that the wind carries around the planet.

> ## WORDS TO KNOW
>
> **pollutant:** something that makes the air, water, or soil dirty and damages the environment.
>
> **livestock:** animals raised for food and other products.

One of the worst examples in history happened in 1815, when the Mount Tambora volcano in the Indian Ocean erupted. Thick ash and dust from the volcano hid the sun and lowered the earth's temperatures by 5 degrees Fahrenheit (15 degrees Celsius). The next year became known as the "Year Without Summer." Crops didn't grow and **livestock** died in Europe and North America.

The second kind of air pollution is created by people. Everything we burn, such as wood, coal, and gasoline, puts pollutants such as the gas carbon monoxide into the air. Spray paints, glues, hairspray, and other chemical products contain pollutants too.

In 2013, hundreds of fires on the Indonesian island of Sumatra burned out of control for weeks. The fires had been set by plantation owners to clear the land. The wind carried the smoke to the neighboring countries of Malaysia and Singapore.

Air pollution isn't a new problem. There have been reports of air pollution for hundreds of years. In 1273, British King Edward I worried about the smoky London air. He tried to stop his people from burning sea coal because it created clouds of smoke. But people kept burning it anyway since wood was more expensive.

THEN & NOW

On December 31, 1970, President Richard Nixon signed the Clean Air Act to improve the health of people and the environment.

Forty years later, the Clean Air Act is believed to have prevented thousands of deaths by reducing air pollution.

The **Industrial Revolution** was a time when **industries** and **manufacturing** of goods grew quickly during the 1800s and 1900s. Pollution grew as factory chimneys belched out black smoke.

This smoke created a thick fog of pollutants so poisonous that many people died. A London doctor named Harold Des Voeux combined the words smoke and fog to invent the word **smog**.

WORDS TO KNOW

Industrial Revolution: the name of the period of time that started in England in the late 1700s when people started using machines to make things in large factories.

industry: the production of goods in factories.

manufacturing: to make large quantities of products in factories using machines.

smog: fog combined with smoke or other pollutants.

power station: a place that generates electrical power.

In December 1952, nearly 4,000 people died from the smog that covered London for days. The smog was so thick that people couldn't see their feet! Once again, burning coal was to blame. After the "Great Smog," Great Britain passed the Clean Air Act in 1956. It moved **power stations** and polluting industries out of areas where a lot of people lived.

LOS ANGELES SMOG

Smog isn't something that has happened only in European history. Los Angeles, California, is nicknamed the "Smog Capital of the World." Brown skies over the San Fernando Valley outside of Los Angeles were first noted in 1943. On days when the skies were thick with smog, people tried to stay inside. No one wanted to breathe in the filthy air that made them cough and their eyes water. It took scientists a few years to realize that **fumes** from cars and buses were causing the pollution.

WORDS TO KNOW

fumes: gas, smoke, or vapor that is dangerous to inhale.

The mountains that surround Los Angeles block pollution so it can't move out. In addition, warm California weather acts like a lid, holding the pollution in. The pollutants can only escape to the upper atmosphere in the evening, when temperatures cool off. Many laws have been passed to try to lower the amount of air pollutants in southern California.

THE OZONE

You've probably seen movies with knights holding up enormous shields to protect themselves. Ozone is like a shield, but it's not made of metal. Almost all of the ozone is in the stratosphere, 6 to 31 miles (10 to 50 kilometers) above the earth. Ozone is a good thing in the stratosphere because it protects us from some of the sun's damaging **ultraviolet** rays.

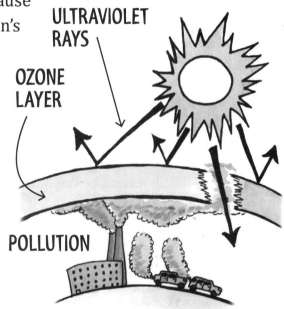

ULTRAVIOLET RAYS

OZONE LAYER

POLLUTION

WORDS TO KNOW

ultraviolet: invisible energy produced by the sun.

aerosol: a substance contained under **pressure** and released by a gas as a spray.

pressure: the force that pushes on any object.

But if ozone gets near the surface of the earth, in the troposphere, it is a pollutant. It can damage plants and people's lungs and even cause rubber to crack. What creates ozone in the troposphere? Chemicals in car exhaust, from factories, and in certain kinds of **aerosol** sprays. On hot days, ozone mixes with sunlight to form ozone fog. In the 1970s, scientists began studying how different chemicals affect the ozone layer. One of these chemicals is chlorofluorocarbons (CFCs). These are found in items such as air conditioning units and aerosol cans.

Scientists discovered that ultraviolet rays break down CFCs into harmful gases such as chlorine. Chlorine causes the protective ozone layer in the stratosphere to thin.

In 1987, many countries, including the United States, signed the Montreal Protocol on Substances that Deplete the Ozone. As of 2012, nearly 200 countries had signed it. Even though these countries agreed to stop using CFCs, scientists believe it will take more than 50 years for chlorine levels to return to normal.

KEEP THE AIR CLEAN

You might not drive a car yet, but there are still many things you can do to keep the air clean.

* Walk, ride your bike, or skateboard to school whenever possible.

* Encourage your family to recycle plastic, paper, glass, and aluminum. This conserves energy and reduces pollutants put into the air.

* Ask your parents not to use the drive-thru window at the bank or fast food restaurant. Park the family car and go inside to do your business or pick up your order. That way you won't sit there in line with your car idling. Can you think of other times or places you can shut off the car while you're waiting?

* If you're in charge of mowing the lawn, ask your parents to switch from a gas-powered mower to one that creates less pollution, such as a push mower.

MAKE A CLEAN AIR POSTER

In this activity, you are going to design a poster promoting clean methods of transportation. Walking, cycling, or carpooling put less pollutants into the air. Ask permission to put your poster up at school or in another public place.

1 Flatten out a cereal box by opening it up along the seams.

2 Using your scissors, cut off the sides so that you are left with two rectangles. Choose one for the base of your poster.

3 Think of a catchy **slogan** for the poster to get people's attention.

4 Cut out images from a magazine or use your markers or pencils to design a poster.

THINGS TO TRY: Take a poll among your friends to see which form of transportation is most popular for getting to school. Make a plan with your friends to try a more air–friendly way to get to school.

SUPPLIES

- ⚙ cereal box
- ⚙ scissors
- ⚙ magazines
- ⚙ markers or colored pencils
- ⚙ glue

WORDS TO KNOW

slogan: a phrase used in advertising that is easy to remember.

CLEAN AIR EXPERIMENT

You have read a lot about air pollution in this chapter. Now it's time to test the air inside and outside your home or school. In this experiment, the petroleum jelly will attract visible air pollutants.

1 Before beginning, start a scientific method worksheet like the one shown below. The scientific method is the way scientists ask questions and find answers. Choose a notebook to use as your science notebook for the activities in this book.

SUPPLIES

- ✺ notebook
- ✺ pencil
- ✺ 4 index cards (or cut a paper file folder)
- ✺ petroleum jelly
- ✺ tape
- ✺ magnifying glass

SCIENTIFIC METHOD WORKSHEET

QUESTIONS: What is the point of this activity? What am I trying to find out? What problem am I trying to solve?

EQUIPMENT: What did I use?

METHOD: What did I do?

HYPOTHESIS/PREDICTIONS: What do I think will happen?

RESULTS: What actually happened? Why?

2 Which card do you think will have the most air pollutants on it and why? Write down your hypothesis. This is your idea that explains what will happen.

3 Label one card "Inside Experiment 1" and a second card "Inside Experiment 2." Label the other two cards "Outside Experiment 1" and "Outside Experiment 2." Spread petroleum jelly on the cards.

4 Place one card on the inside of a window and the second card on the outside of the window. Secure them in place with tape. Place the second set of cards on a different window and secure with tape.

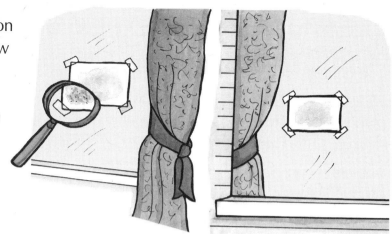

5 Using a magnifying glass, check your cards every day for a week and record your results in your notebook.

THINGS TO THINK ABOUT: How did your results compare to your hypothesis? A particle is a very tiny piece of something. What do you think is the main source of particle pollution inside your home? What do you think is the main source of particle pollution outside your home?

THINGS TO TRY: Tape new cards on a car or a bicycle. You can also tape a set of cards on windows at your school. Do you notice anything different? Why might these results be different?

DID YOU KNOW?

In the Netherlands, scientists have invented air-purifying pavement. It is sprayed with titanium oxide, which gives it the ability to cut air pollution in half. The pavement works by removing pollutants from the air and turning them into harmless chemicals.

CREATING OXYGEN EXPERIMENT

In the eighteenth century, a scientist named Jan Ingenhousz carried out underwater experiments with plants. He wanted to investigate how plants produce oxygen. In this activity, you are going to conduct a similar experiment to see for yourself how plants produce oxygen.

SUPPLIES

- ❂ science notebook
- ❂ pencil
- ❂ Elodea plants (water plants)
- ❂ 2 large jars with lids
- ❂ tap water

1 Start a scientific method worksheet in your science notebook and write down your hypothesis. Which plant do you think will produce more oxygen? Why?

2 Place a large piece of Elodea plant in the bottom of each jar, fill with water, and screw the lids on tightly.

3 Place one jar in a window with a lot of sunlight. Place the other jar in a darkened room or closet.

4 After some time, check on your plants and record your results.

WHAT IS HAPPENING? The tiny bubbles in the water are the oxygen produced by the Elodea. In order for plants to produce oxygen, they need light. Your Elodea placed in the sunny room had access to more energy than the plant in the dark room, so it produced oxygen. What would happen if you tried this experiment with distilled water, which contains no carbon dioxide? What would happen if the Elodea plant was placed directly next to an artificial light source, such as a lamp? Would this increase the rate of photosynthesis? Why or why not?

IT'S ACTIVITY TIME!

VOC EXPERIMENT

You've learned that the chemicals called CFCs used to be part of appliances and aerosol cans. This was before we discovered they hurt the earth's atmosphere. CFCs are a kind of **volatile organic compound (VOC)**. Other kinds of VOCs are commonly found in products around the house, such as paint and paint thinner, furniture polish, rubbing alcohol, nail polish, hair spray, perfume, dry cleaned clothes, glue, moth balls, and pesticides. In this experiment, you are going to look for products with VOCs in your home. **NOTE: Ask an adult to supervise if you use the Internet.**

WORDS TO KNOW

volatile organic compound (VOC): a kind of chemical that can be harmful to humans and the environment.

1 Before beginning, start a scientific method worksheet in your science notebook and write down a hypothesis. Your hypothesis should state which room you think will have the most products containing VOCs and why.

2 Divide your paper into columns, one for each room you are going to investigate. Explore each room and write down the products you find in the appropriate column.

ROOM 1	ROOM 2	ROOM 3	ROOM 4

3 When you have looked in all the rooms, create a bar graph with your results. For help with, this go to **nces.ed.gov/nceskids/createagraph**.

THINGS TO THINK ABOUT: How did your results compare to your original hypothesis? Which room had the most VOC products? Why do you think this was? What air-friendly products could you replace VOC products with?

WONDERFUL WATER

Do you have a nickname? The earth does. It's called the "blue planet" because 71 percent of the earth is covered in water. Most of this water is found in the oceans—the Atlantic, Pacific, Indian, Arctic, and Southern oceans.

Plain water in a glass might be colorless, tasteless, and have no smell, but without it there would be no life on earth. We all need water to stay alive. We swim and play in water and we travel by it. We also use its energy for power.

You might think that there is so much water that we could never run out of it, but only some of the earth's water can be used by humans. This is because most of the earth's water is salt water. If all of the water in the world could fit into a 4-quart (3.7-liter) container, how much of it do you think would be freshwater that we could drink? The answer is a tablespoon!

VS.

Only 2½ percent of the earth's water is freshwater. This is what you pour yourself when you need a cool drink after playing outside. But not even all of the earth's freshwater is easy for people to use. Some freshwater is stored deep underground or frozen in ice caps and **glaciers**.

WORDS TO KNOW

glacier: a large area of ice and snow.

JUST FOR LAUGHS

WHAT SPORT IS WATER GOOD AT IN SCHOOL?

Running!

WATER CYCLE

Earth's water is recycled again and again. This is why the amount of water on the earth has remained the same for 2 billion years. That's right—the water you drink might have flowed by the pyramids in ancient Egypt!

The **water cycle** is happening all around you! The sun powers the water cycle by heating up water **molecules**. This heat breaks down the **bonds** that hold the water molecules together. It changes liquid water into a gas called water vapor. This is how the water cycle begins. Water can also change from a solid to a liquid, from ice into rain.

During the water cycle, bodies of water such as lakes and ponds absorb the sun's energy. Some of the water **evaporates**. Most evaporation takes place over oceans because they cover such a huge area of the earth.

WORDS TO KNOW

water cycle: the continuous movement of water from the earth to the clouds and back to earth again.

molecule: the smallest amount of something.

bond: a force that holds two things together.

evaporate: when a liquid turns into a vapor.

condense: when a vapor turns into a liquid.

precipitation: falling moisture in the form of rain, sleet, snow, and hail.

When water vapor enters the atmosphere, it cools or **condenses** into droplets. During condensation, the droplets become clouds. When the water droplets become heavy enough, it's time to get out your umbrella or shovel. The droplets will fall as rain or snow, depending on the temperature. This is called **precipitation**.

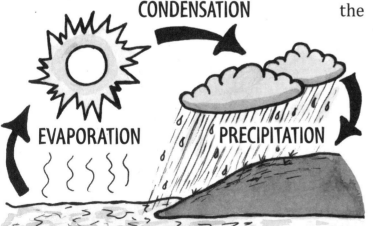

CONDENSATION

EVAPORATION   PRECIPITATION

DID YOU KNOW?

Americans use roughly 80 to 100 gallons (320 to 400 liters) of water per person each day! Most of this water is used to grow the fruits and vegetables you eat and to make the clothes you wear.

Water that falls on the ground can flow into a river or an ocean. It can flow into lakes and ponds. Or it can move through the soil and rocks to **reservoirs** deep underground. Water can remain underground for a long time.

WORDS TO KNOW

reservoir: a body of water that is stored for future use. It can be natural or man-made.

drought: a long period of time with little or no rain.

Aboriginal: the first people who lived in Australia.

WATER MYTHOLOGY

Long ago, people didn't understand why it rained or why there were **droughts**. To explain these mysterious events, they made up stories. Knowing what we know about rain and droughts today, we might find these stories funny. In a famous **Aboriginal** tale, Tiddalik, a giant frog, doesn't want to go thirsty during the dry season. So Tiddalik drinks all the water he can find.

"burp!"

When the other animals learn of his plan they grow angry. They try to make the frog laugh so that he will spit out the water. Once he laughs, water fills the land and there is enough for everyone. As for Tiddalik, legend has it he turned to stone!

WATER AND YOU

Did you know that more than half of your body is water? Without it, your body wouldn't work. Humans aren't the only ones that need water. Without water, there would be no animals, plants, or any other living thing. Through the process of photosynthesis, plants use water and sunlight to make their own food. Do you eat fruits and vegetables? Plants are an important food source for most people.

WATER POLLUTION

You drink water every day. What if you saw dirt or twigs floating in your glass of water? You wouldn't want to drink it, and it wouldn't be healthy to drink.

Even though we have **water treatment plants** to clean water before we drink it, there is still polluted water. Pollutants such as **pesticides**, **fertilizers**, or waste cause changes in ecosystems. For example, when fertilizers wash into river and ponds, tiny plants called **algae** can quickly multiply. The algae use all the oxygen in the water. When this happens, the other plants and fish die.

WORDS TO KNOW

water treatment plant: a place where water is cleaned.

pesticide: a chemical used to kill pests, such as insects.

fertilizer: any substance put on land to help crops grow better.

algae: a simple organism found in water. It is like a plant but does not have roots, stems, or leaves.

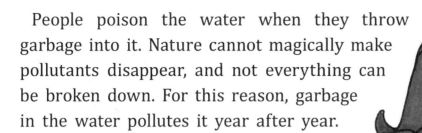

People poison the water when they throw garbage into it. Nature cannot magically make pollutants disappear, and not everything can be broken down. For this reason, garbage in the water pollutes it year after year.

ACID RAIN

Acid rain is precipitation mixed with chemicals such as sulfur dioxide and nitrogen oxide. These colorless gases or liquids get in the air and fall with the rain. Volcanoes and forest fire smoke create acidic gases. People also create acidic gases when they burn fossil fuels for energy.

On land, acid rain can weaken and kill trees and plants. These trees and plants are part of the **food chain**. What happens when they die? The animals that live in these forests don't have enough food to eat.

The same is true when acid rain falls into water sources. Although acid lakes look clear, they are not clean. They look this way because all the living things have died from the high levels of acid. In the Canadian province of Nova Scotia, scientists believe that one quarter of freshwater fish have been killed due to acid rain.

WORDS TO KNOW

acid rain: precipitation that has been polluted by acid.

food chain: the feeding relationship between plants and animals in an environment.

CALCULATE YOUR WATER FOOTPRINT

Discover how much water you use each day. The total amount is called your water footprint.

1 Start a scientific method worksheet. How much water do you think you use each day? Do some people in your family use more water than others?

2 Divide a sheet of paper into five columns. Label each column with one of the following phrases: brushing your teeth, taking a shower, flushing the toilet, running the dishwasher, and washing your face.

SUPPLIES

- ✪ science notebook
- ✪ pencil
- ✪ ruler
- ✪ empty gallon jug
- ✪ faucet
- ✪ stopwatch

BRUSHING YOUR TEETH	TAKING A SHOWER	FLUSHING THE TOILET	RUNNING THE DISHWASHER	WASHING YOUR FACE
ESTIMATE:	ESTIMATE:	ESTIMATE:	ESTIMATE:	ESTIMATE:
ACTUAL:	ACTUAL:	ACTUAL:	ACTUAL:	ACTUAL:

3 Fill the jug with water and see how long it takes to fill it. Using the gallon jug as your unit of measure, write down estimates for how much water you think you use under each of your columns.

4 Now use a stopwatch to time yourself as you brush your teeth.

5 Next, place the gallon jug under a tap and run it the same amount of time. How did your estimate compare with your test result? Are your estimates for the other activities correct?

6 Ask an adult if you can go online and visit **environment.nationalgeographic.com/ environment/freshwater/change-the-course/ water-footprint-calculator**. This site can help you calculate your water footprint, including the amounts used to produce what you wear and eat.

THINGS TO THINK ABOUT: Did any activities go over your estimate? If so, how could you lower it? Can you think of ways to reuse the water you used in this activity? Do you have plants you can water? Dishes to wash?

HELP CONSERVE WATER

Here are some ways to help conserve water and keep it clean.

* Turn off the tap when you brush your teeth in the morning and at night.
* Only run the dishwasher when it's full.
* Collect and use rainwater for the garden.
* Drink tap water instead of bottled water.
* Don't pour oil or grease down storm drains.
* After a day at the beach or lake, pick up all your litter.

WATER WORD GAME

Fill in the blanks with words from the glossary or text. After you have finished, read your story!

noun: a person, place, or thing.
plural noun: more than one person, place, or thing.
adjective: a word that modifies a noun.
verb: an action word.
adverb: a word that modifies a verb.

_____ has an important _____ to do in the _____ town of
YOUR NAME   NOUN   ADJECTIVE
_____, where he/she had been put in charge of _____ . In this new and
NOUN   NOUN
exciting role, _____ would have to _____ and _____ water. The
                    YOUR NAME   VERB   VERB
_____ people know water is a _____ _____ but they don't
ADJECTIVE   ADJECTIVE   NOUN
know how to get _____. When _____ arrives in town, he/she is shocked
                        VERB   YOUR NAME
to see sprinklers _____, taps _____, and people _____ garbage into
                          VERB   VERB   VERB
lakes and streams. Instead of sprinklers, the people are told to use _____ to collect
                                                                               NOUN
rainwater. Someone suggests using old _____ barrels, which _____ from
                                                ADJECTIVE   VERB
schools. Next, the townspeople fix leaky taps. They can save water at home by taking a
_____ instead of a _____. They are also taught to fill a _____ bottle
NOUN   NOUN   NOUN
with _____, _____, and pebbles and place it in the toilet tank to use less
        NOUN   NOUN
water per flush. But the work is not done yet. The townspeople must _____ the
                                                                               VERB
_____ polluted lakes and _____. They _____ banks of the
ADVERB   NOUN   VERB
_____ and _____. They collect _____ of trash. At local campgrounds
NOUN   NOUN   NUMBER
and beaches, a recycling program is _____. Now picnickers and beach goers place
                                            VERB
their _____ in _____. Eventually, _____ realize that small acts can
        NOUN   NOUN   NOUN
make a big _____. You are not the only Enviro-hero. You have made the town's
                NOUN
_____ into _____ too.
NOUN   NOUN

DEHYDRATION EXPERIMENT

The human body can go nearly an entire month without food. But it can survive only between five and seven days without water. In this experiment, you are going to see what happens when your body loses water. **CAUTION: This activity requires the use of a knife, so ask an adult to supervise.**

SUPPLIES

- apple
- vegetable peeler
- knife
- science notebook
- pencil
- string
- scissors

1 Peel off the apple skin and put it in a composter.

2 Next, cut an apple slice. Use the pencil to make a tracing of the apple slice in your science notebook.

3 Make a hole at one end of the apple slice with your pencil. Cut off a length of string and tie the string through the hole. Hang up the apple.

4 What happens? How long does it take for the apple slice to dry out? Record your observations once or twice a day in your science notebook.

5 After the slice has dried out, make another tracing of the slice and compare it to your original.

THINGS TO THINK ABOUT: Would your results be different if the apple slice was in a cool room versus a hot room? What if it was in direct sunlight versus the shade?

PURIFYING WATER EXPERIMENT

As the earth's water travels from the oceans to the sky and then back to the earth, rocks, salt, or sand are filtered out. In this experiment, you are going to discover how the water cycle purifies water.

1 Start a scientific method worksheet in your science notebook and write down your hypothesis. Do you think the water collected in the cup will be purified?

2 Pour 2 cups (475 milliliters) of dirt into the glass bowl and then stir in the water.

3 Place the drinking glass right side up in the center of the bowl. It should be tall enough so that its opening is above the water's surface. But the top of the drinking glass should be below the top of the bowl.

4 Put the bowl on a flat surface in direct sunlight and cover it tightly with plastic wrap. Place a rock on the plastic directly over the center of the drinking glass.

SUPPLIES

- science notebook
- pencil
- 4 cups water (1 liter)
- large mixing bowl and spoon
- 2 cups dirt or sand (475 milliliters)
- drinking glass
- plastic wrap
- rock
- sunny spot

THEN & NOW

Before the Clean Water Act became law in 1972, many American rivers were polluted with garbage.

The quality of water in America has improved. Polluted waterways are now recovering.

5 After several hours have passed, look in the bowl and observe what is in the glass.

6 Repeat this experiment, but this time, add a small amount of food coloring to the water.

THINGS TO THINK ABOUT: Can you think of two examples of condensation on earth? What do you think would happen in your experiment if there was no plastic wrap?

WHAT IS HAPPENING? When energy from the sun warms the water, the water molecules become vapor. This is the process of evaporation. The water vapor hits the plastic and condenses into liquid. The water droplets drop into the glass. This is the water cycle!

WATER-SAVING SHOWER

The average household could use 20,000 to 32,000 fewer gallons (76,000 to 121,000 liters) of water per year thanks to a new invention that recirculates used water. Scientist Peter Brewin's Water Recycling Shower captures and cleans 70 percent of the water used in a shower. It is hoped that this invention will be put to use in drought and disaster areas.

SUPER SOIL

There is an important natural resource right beneath your feet. Sometimes it is hidden under roads, sidewalks, or buildings. One-fourth of all living species call this natural resource home, including both plants and animals. What is this natural resource? It's soil!

It's easy to call soil dirt, but soil is much more than just dirt. Dirt is what you find on your pants after sliding into home plate. Soil is a rich mixture of **organic matter**, clay, and rock particles.

WORDS TO KNOW

organic matter: decaying plants and animals that give soil its nutrients.

Although soil covers only 10 percent of the earth, it performs many important jobs. Soil holds **nutrients** and water. This is why we grow our food in soil and why plants and animals call it home.

WORDS TO KNOW

nutrients: substances in food and soil that living things need to live and grow.

erosion: the gradual wearing away of rock or soil by water and wind.

It takes thousands of years to produce just 1 inch of soil. About 95 percent of soil is tiny pieces of crushed rocks, clay, and sand called minerals. **Erosion** breaks down rocks into these tiny pieces. Organic matter such as leaves, dead plants, and animals break down, too, and mix in with the minerals.

Two other natural resources, air and water, fill the spaces between the minerals. This makes it possible for plants and animals to live in the soil. A super gardener with no arms, legs, or eyes also makes the soil a perfect environment for plants and animals. Can you guess what organism this is?

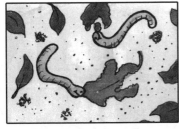 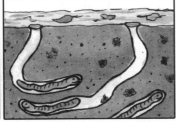 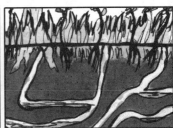

Worms eat and break down organic matter, leaving behind waste called worm castings. These are a source of nutrients for plants. When worms tunnel through the ground, they mix the soil and create space for water and air. This allows plant roots to grow more easily.

LAYERS OF SOIL

Soil is made up of layers. The top layer is the **topsoil**. This layer is full of nutrients that help seeds to sprout and plant roots to grow. Plants provide food and shelter for the many animals that live in the topsoil. Tiny organisms called **decomposers** break down **decaying** plants and animals. The organic matter they leave behind is called **humus**.

> # WORDS TO KNOW
>
> **topsoil:** the upper layer of soil.
>
> **decomposers:** organisms such as ants, worms, and fungi that break down wastes, dead plants, and dead animals. Fungi are organisms such as mold and mushrooms.
>
> **decay:** to rot.
>
> **humus:** soil formed from decaying leaves and organisms.
>
> **subsoil:** the layer of soil beneath the topsoil.
>
> **bedrock:** the solid rock below the subsoil.

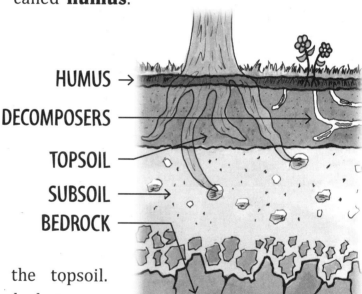

HUMUS →
DECOMPOSERS
TOPSOIL
SUBSOIL
BEDROCK

The **subsoil** is below the topsoil. Subsoil has lots of minerals but very little humus. In between the minerals are pockets of water and air. Some plant roots make their way into the subsoil in search of water. Beneath the subsoil are layers of rock called **bedrock**.

SOIL TYPES

Around the world there are many different types of soil. Desert soil covers about one-fifth of the earth. It is dry and sandy. It contains very little organic matter and doesn't hold water well.

Have you ever drained noodles with a **sieve**? That's how water moves through sand.

WORDS TO KNOW

sieve: a bowl or basket with lots of small holes in it.

Clay is another type of soil. It's made up of a lot of water and only a little air, which is why it's great for making tiles, pottery, and bricks. Sand is used in plaster, concrete, and clay bricks to make them stronger. The tallest brick skyscraper in the world is New York City's Chrysler Building. It's made of clay bricks.

JUST FOR LAUGHS

WHY WERE THE KIDS DIGGING IN THE DIRT?

Because they dug it!

Soil formed from volcanic ash is light, fluffy, and high in minerals. This soil is called loam. It is full of water, air, and organic matter with nutrients, making it good for growing crops.

WHO WAS ALDO LEOPOLD?

Aldo Leopold was a conservationist who wrote about the importance of living in harmony with the land. In 1935, he helped found the Wilderness Society, which is dedicated to protecting wilderness areas.

SOIL POLLUTION

Soil performs many important jobs, but this resource is threatened by pollution. Waste from farms, such as pesticides, and factories, such as lead and mercury, pollute the soil. Rainwater can wash road salt or oils into the soil.

PRODUCE

WORDS TO KNOW

groundwater: water found in cracks or spaces beneath the surface of the earth.

contaminate: to pollute or make dirty.

landfill: a huge area of land where trash gets buried.

When pollutants end up in the soil, a damaging chain reaction begins. Both the plants growing in the soil and the **groundwater** become **contaminated**. This harms animals and insects. Food grown in polluted soil can make people sick.

DID YOU KNOW?

As **landfill** waste breaks down, it releases a harmful greenhouse gas called methane. A new project will allow the U.S. Marine Corps Air Station Miramar in California to use methane gas from a nearby landfill to generate half of its electricity. This will keep the methane from polluting the air. It will also reduce the amount of nonrenewable resources needed to produce electricity for the air station.

EROSION

According to scientists, the world is losing **fertile** soil faster than it can be replaced.

Erosion is a natural process. But **overgrazing** and **deforestation** strip the soil of trees and other plants. Without this protection, the soil erodes—it can blow or wash away. Over time, the soil loses nutrients and nothing will grow in it. The soil may become more sandy, like a desert. This is called **desertification**. Each year, so much farmable land becomes desert that it could fill the state of Pennsylvania!

Soil erosion also pollutes rivers and streams. When there are fewer plants, soil and polluted water flows straight off the land. Pollutants can harm **marine** habitats. In warm waters such as the Florida Keys, **sediment** covers the coral reef and blocks the sunlight from reaching it. The coral and sea grass can't grow without sun.

WORDS TO KNOW

fertile: good for growing crops.

overgraze: when animals eat all of the plants in an area.

deforestation: when trees are cut down or burned to clear the land.

desertification: when farmable land turns into desert.

marine: found in the ocean.

sediment: bits of rock, sand, or dirt that have been carried to a place by water and wind.

WATER ABSORBS

WATER RUNS OFF

DUST BOWL

One of the worst examples of erosion in the United States happened in the Midwestern states in the 1930s. This area was called the Dust Bowl after powerful dust storms destroyed the farmland. In the years before the storms, farmers plowed up grasses that protected the soil and planted the same crops year after year. This prevented new nutrients from entering the soil.

Without grasses and nutrients, drought and dust storms destroyed the topsoil. Many people lost their farms. Farmers learned to plant different crops each year to keep the soil nutrient-rich. They also planted trees as wind breaks.

KEEPING SOIL HEALTHY

Without soil, where would we grow our food? There are lots of creative ways you can keep soil healthy.

* Never use chemicals to get rid of garden pests.

* Organize a trash cleanup at a local park or school in your community.

* Minimize your family's garbage by **composting** kitchen waste.

* Rotate what you plant in the vegetable garden each year. Fertilize with your compost!

* Bring reusable lunch containers to school.

* Plant a tree each June 17. This is World Day to Combat Desertification.

WORDS TO KNOW

compost: to recycle food scraps and vegetation and put them back in the soil.

48

MAKE A MINI COMPOST BIN

Compost is organic matter that can be added to soil as fertilizer. You can make you own compost! Compost uses brown waste, such as shredded newspapers, and green waste, such as fruit and vegetable leftovers. Avoid putting meat, dairy, or oils in your composter, as they slow down the process of decay.

1 Cut the top off a milk carton. You can cover the outside of the carton with plain paper and decorate it with crayons or markers.

2 Collect some brown and green organic waste, such as newspaper scraps, potato peels, and apple cores. Add some of it to your container. Sprinkle this layer with soil.

3 Repeat until your container is three-quarters full. Then cover the top with foil to prevent moisture from escaping.

4 Stir the compost every day. Add a bit of water if you see it drying out. Write down your observations during a four-week period.

WHAT IS HAPPENING? Tiny decomposers called fungi work together to break down material in the composter. Every time you stir the compost, you are allowing air to reach into different areas.

SUPPLIES

- milk carton
- scissors
- paper
- tape
- crayons/markers
- green and brown compost
- soil
- foil
- water

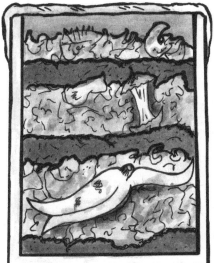

BUILD AN EROSION MODEL

What happens to soil when all the trees and other plants are cleared away for farmland? Or when cattle eat all the grass on the land? Soil needs plants growing in it to hold it there. If the plants and grass are gone, the soil can erode. Now you can see erosion in action.

SUPPLIES

- ✪ science notebook
- ✪ pencil
- ✪ plastic paint tray
- ✪ soil
- ✪ popsicle sticks
- ✪ pebbles
- ✪ moss or grass
- ✪ measuring cup
- ✪ water

1 Start a scientific method worksheet to organize your experiment. Write down a hypothesis. Which tray do you think will erode more, the one covered with popsicle-stick trees and grass or the tray with no coverings? Why?

2 Prepare your tray by pouring a layer of soil evenly over the surface. Pack it down with your hands.

3 Push popsicle sticks, moss, grass, and pebbles into the soil. Drag your fingers through the soil to create deep pathways for the water.

4 Slowly pour ½ cup (120 milliliters) of water all over the soil and observe what happens. How much water flows into the pathways?

5 Clean everything off the tray. Sprinkle a layer of soil evenly over the tray and drag your fingers through the soil to create deep pathways again. Slowly pour the same amount of water and observe what happens.

THINGS TO THINK ABOUT: What would happen if the soil was mixed with sand? What if you put one end of the paint tray on a book?

SEEDLING EXPERIMENT

Plants need sunlight, water, and healthy soil to grow. By creating six mini planters, you can discover which type of soil is best to grow plants in and why.

1 Start a scientific method worksheet in your science notebook to organize your experiment. What is your hypothesis?

2 Crack three eggs in half and save the eggs for breakfast! Rinse the six half eggshells, taking care not to break them.

3 Using the marker, write "topsoil" on two of the eggshells. Repeat this step for "sand" and "clay." You can also decorate the shells with colored markers.

4 Place the clean shells in an egg carton. Fill the eggshells marked topsoil with topsoil. Repeat this step for sand and clay.

5 Place a few seeds in each egg shell. Water according to the instructions on seed packet.

6 Record your results during the next few weeks. Which type of soil grows the healthiest plants?

SUPPLIES

- science notebook
- 3 eggs
- waterproof markers
- egg container
- ¼ cup each topsoil, sand, and clay (60 milliliters)
- seeds
- water

THINGS TO TRY: Transfer your seedlings to a larger garden. The eggshells will break down naturally and add important nutrients to the soil.

DESERTIFICATION EXPERIMENT

More than 900 million people live in countries affected by desertification. See how desertification affects soil temperatures in this activity.

1 Fill two pails with equal amounts of sand.

2 Place the first pail in a shady spot and use your thermometer to take the temperature of the sand.

3 Place the second pail in a sunny spot and use your thermometer to take the temperature of the sand.

4 After 30 minutes, take another reading and record this information. Do this three more times, every 30 minutes, so that you have four results per pail.

5 Take your results and create a line graph. Ask a parent to help you go online and create your graph at **nces.ed.gov/nceskids/createagraph**.

SUPPLIES

- ❀ 2 plastic pails
- ❀ sand
- ❀ thermometer
- ❀ science notebook
- ❀ pencil

DID YOU KNOW?

In the United States, each state has an official flower. Did you know that each state also has an official soil? With an adult's permission, explore state soils online at the Smithsonian web site: forces.si.edu/soils/interactive/statesoils.

MIGHTY MINERALS

What do a soccer ball, your body, and a toaster have in common? They are all made with minerals. Almost everything on earth, from fruits and vegetables to the sidewalk in front of your home—even you—would not exist without minerals.

A mineral is a natural solid that is not living. It was never alive. No matter where you find a particular mineral, it will always have the same **crystal** structure. Rocks contain two or more different minerals. The structure of a rock depends on the minerals in it and how it was formed.

WORDS TO KNOW

crystal: a solid with its molecules arranged in a repeated pattern.

Minerals form from heat and pressure in the earth's **crust** over millions of years. Our planet is home to almost 4,000 different minerals. Minerals are natural resources that can be grouped as metals, nonmetals, or gemstones.

METALS

What has a shiny surface and allows heat and electricity to flow through it? Metals, such as copper, gold, and silver. These metals are found in **ore**. Some ores contain just one metal, such as gold or silver. But most metals, such as **iron** and tin, are mixed with other minerals.

COPPER: This metal has been used to make weapons, tools, and jewelry since 9000 BCE. Today, screws, door hinges, and even roofs are made of copper. Since copper can **conduct** heat and electricity, it's used for electrical components such as wire. Do you have copper in your pocket right now? An American penny is about 3 percent copper. Before 1837, pennies were 100 percent copper.

> # WORDS TO KNOW
>
> **crust:** the earth's outer layer.
>
> **ore:** a naturally occurring mineral that contains metal.
>
> **iron:** a strong, hard, magnetic metal.
>
> **conduct:** to transfer something.

DID YOU KNOW?

Everyday, millions of tin cans are made. Though they are called tin cans, they are mostly made of steel, which is made from iron. The outside of the can is tin to protect the steel from rusting.

CAN IRON CLEAN UP OIL SPILLS?

What happens when oil spills into the ocean after an accident? The oil poisons birds, fish, and other animals in the water. Researchers at the Massachusetts Institute of Technology want to mix oil with tiny, water-repellent particles that contain iron. If the oil ever spills, then it could be separated from the water using magnets.

GOLD: There is something special about gold. One of the most famous gold creations comes from 1223 BCE. It is the solid gold funeral mask of Egypt's King Tutankhamen. Later, around 564 BCE, gold began to be used as money. In the 1850s, gold found in the American River in California started a rush to the West Coast of the United States called the Gold Rush.

Today, gold is also used in medicine and computers and on satellites. In the future, it might be used to clean water. Scientist Michael Wong is developing a detergent with tiny gold particles that can break down **toxic** chemicals in groundwater.

WORDS TO KNOW

toxic: poisonous.

NONMETALS

Minerals that are nonmetals do not shine like a metal. These dull minerals are used to make products such as bricks, glass, or floor tiles. Salt and gypsum are examples of nonmetallic minerals.

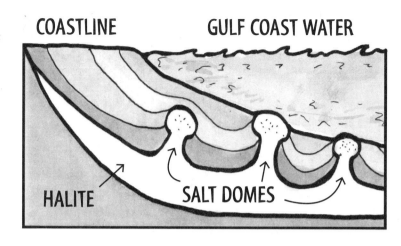

COASTLINE   **GULF COAST WATER**

HALITE   **SALT DOMES**

SALT: Can you think of something salty that you like to eat? Salt comes from a mineral called halite. Salt deposits can be found both deep underground and above ground. Along the Gulf Coast of Texas and Louisiana, massive mushroom-shaped deposits of salt, called salt domes, formed millions of years ago where seas once flowed.

But the biggest source of salt is the ocean. What if you could take out all the salt in ocean water? It could cover all the land on the earth with a layer as thick as the height of a 40-story building!

WORDS TO KNOW

translucent: allowing some light to pass through.

People use salt in food and on roads to melt snow and ice. Salt also produces chlorine, used in cleaning products, medicine, cell phones, and even scuba suits.

GYPSUM: Gypsum is a beautiful, soft white, **translucent** mineral. To make a cast for a broken arm or leg, doctors soak bandages in a plaster made with gypsum. After a few hours, the gypsum hardens.

A variation of gypsum is alabaster. Artists have used alabaster for thousands of years to create sculptures, chess pieces, and other beautiful objects. The Greeks and Romans admired its marble-like qualities and used it for vases.

GEMSTONES

Diamonds, rubies, and emeralds are examples of gemstones. Most are found deep beneath the earth, where they began forming billions of years ago. Gems are cut and polished, then used in jewelry such as rings and necklaces. You can see many colors, sizes, and shapes of gems in jewelry stores.

Gems are popular because they are so beautiful, and they are very hard. The diamond is the hardest material known to us. Diamonds are used for drilling and cutting.

EXTRACTING METALS

Sometimes minerals such as diamonds or gold can be above the ground, but usually you have to dig them up. How do you get minerals out of the ground?

A mine is a series of tunnels dug into the ground to the location of a mineral deposit. After ore is dug up, metals have to be **extracted** from the ore. Sometimes high heat or electricity is used to release metal from rocks.

WORDS TO KNOW

extract: to remove or take out by effort or force.

At some large mines, mounds of dirt as high as the Great Pyramid in Egypt are removed each day. What do you think happens to this waste? Abandoned mines often leave huge holes behind, destroy wildlife habitats, and leak waste into water systems. This is why many countries are passing laws to protect the land and the animals living there and to restore lands once mining stops.

GROW A CRYSTAL

Minerals have a crystal structure. This means that the molecules in a crystal are arranged in a pattern that is repeated over and over. There are crystals all around you, such as sugar, salt, and snow. This experiment will teach you how to grow crystals with alum powder.

1 Pour a little hot water into each bowl. Stir some alum into the water. At first it will dissolve. This means it will mix in and disappear. Keep stirring more in until it stops dissolving. It will settle on the bottom.

2 Add a drop of food coloring to three of the bowls. Leave your bowl for a few hours and observe the results.

THINGS TO TRY: Try to grow crystals with salt and compare them with your alum crystals. What would happen if the water was cold?

SUPPLIES

- 4 shallow plastic bowls
- hot water
- alum powder
- spoon
- food coloring

MINIMAL MINERAL WASTE

From watches and jewelry to toothpaste and washing powder, we use minerals every day. Here are some simple things that you can do to conserve this nonrenewable resource.

* Reuse things over and over so that new minerals do not have to be mined to make more things.

* Recycle electronic goods such as computers and cell phones.

* Buy good-quality items so that you can use them for a long time. This will cut down on the amount you throw away.

MAKE A TUTANKHAMEN MASK

Egyptian craftspeople were skilled at using gold. Using markers or crayons, recreate Tutankhamen's gold mask.

1 With permission and help of an adult, research pictures of Tutankhamen's mask online.

2 Roughly sketch the design on paper. Make sure the cobra lines up with your forehead.

3 Color your mask, then carefully cut it out.

4 Hold the mask up to your face and determine where the eyeholes need to be. Cut these out.

5 Punch a hole on either side of the mask and tie string in the holes. Use the ties to hold the mask on your head.

THINGS TO TRY: Make your mask more elaborate by decorating it with gold glitter or sequins.

SUPPLIES
✪ Internet access
✪ paper, 8.5 by 11 inches (21 by 27 centimeters)
✪ yellow, blue, black, grey, and red markers or crayons
✪ scissors
✪ hole punch
✪ string

THEN & NOW

During the Stone Age, which ended more than 4,000 years ago, people made tools from stone.

The average American uses 38,212 pounds (17,332 kilograms) of new minerals each year.

MAKE ROCK COOKIES

Rocks contain two or more different minerals. Without rocks, there would be no limestone for glass, no granite for buildings, and no marble for statues. Make an edible rock cookie and see how it compares to an actual rock or mineral. **NOTE: Have an adult help you with this activity.**

1 Microwave the peanut butter and honey in the mixing bowl until the peanut butter is melted.

2 Mix in the rest of the ingredients and stir until it forms a ball.

3 Cover a baking sheet with wax paper so that the cookies don't stick. With damp hands, take some dough and roll it into a bite-sized ball. Place it on the baking sheet. Repeat until all the dough has been used.

4 Place four of the cookies onto a plate and put the rest in the refrigerator to eat later.

5 On a piece of paper, draw three columns. Label them: "Types of Minerals," "Number of Minerals," and "Mineral Sketch."

JUST FOR LAUGHS

WHY DID THE MINERAL LIKE MUSIC?

He liked to rock out!

SUPPLIES

- microwavable mixing bowl
- measuring cups
- microwave
- spatula
- 1 cup peanut or soy butter (240 milliliters)
- ½ cup honey (120 milliliters)
- ⅓ cup raisins (80 milliliters)
- ¼ cup coconut (60 milliliters)
- ⅓ cup cranberries (80 milliliters)
- ¼ cup chocolate or carob chips (60 milliliters)
- baking sheet
- wax paper
- plate
- refrigerator
- paper and pencil
- toothpicks
- a few rocks and minerals

TYPES OF MINERALS	NUMBER OF MINERALS	MINERAL SKETCH

6 Examine the cookies on the plate. Fill out your chart using one row for your cookie and additional rows for each rock and mineral.

THINGS TO THINK ABOUT: How does your rock cookie differ from your rock and mineral samples? How is it the same? Using toothpicks, can you separate the "minerals" from the "rock" in your cookies?

DID YOU KNOW?

Iron tools dating back to 3000 BCE have been found in what are now Iraq and Egypt. Today, iron is used 20 times more than any other metal. It's a good thing that 5 percent of the earth's crust is iron.

MINERAL HUNT

You can look for minerals in your own home! Which room do you think will have the most minerals? This chart will help you to find out which minerals are in which household objects: **smithsonianeducation.org/ educators/lesson_plans/minerals/lesson3_a.html**. **CAUTION: Be sure to ask an adult's permission before going online.**

SUPPLIES

- ✪ science notebook
- ✪ pencil
- ✪ ruler
- ✪ chart of minerals found in common household objects

1 Start a scientific method worksheet in your science notebook and write down a hypothesis. Which room in your house do you think will contain the most minerals? Why?

2 Go from room to room. Write down as many objects that have minerals in them as you can find.

3 Using the chart from the Smithsonian web site, write down which minerals are found in each object you have listed.

4 Create a line graph out of the results. For examples of a line graph, look at the web link **nces.ed.gov/nceskids/createagraph**.

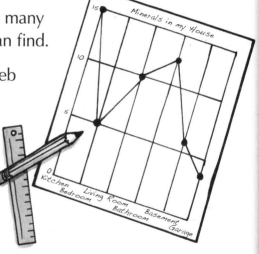

THINGS TO THINK ABOUT:

How did your results compare with your hypothesis? Try doing this experiment at school. How are your results similar to or different from those at home? Or compare two of your favorite sports to discover which uses more minerals.

CREATE A NATURAL PESTICIDE

When you use this natural pesticide, you will know that it isn't going to harm your health. **CAUTION: Have an adult help you with the boiling water and the knife.**

1 Put on plastic gloves so the garlic cloves and chilies don't irritate your hands. **Do not touch your eyes.**

2 With an adult, use the knife to chop the garlic and chilies. Put them in a bowl and add the boiling water.

3 Squeeze a little detergent into the mixture and cover with plastic wrap. Set aside to cool overnight.

4 The next day, place the funnel in the spray bottle. Hold the strainer over the funnel and pour the liquid into the spray bottle. You might want to do this in the sink.

5 Spray your natural pesticide on plant leaves early in the morning to keep pests off of them. When not in use, keep your spray in a cool, dark place.

THINGS TO TRY: Conduct an experiment in your garden. Spray only half of several plants with your pesticide. What results do you get?

SUPPLIES

- plastic gloves
- 4 cloves of garlic
- 6 to 8 red chilies
- cutting board and knife
- bowl
- 4 cups boiling water (1 liter)
- liquid detergent
- plastic wrap
- funnel
- clean spray bottle
- handheld strainer

WHO WAS THEODORE ROOSEVELT?

Theodore Roosevelt, the United State's 26th president (1901–1909), valued the environment. He created the first National Wildlife Refuge and designated many national monuments, including the Grand Canyon.

EXCITING ENERGY

Whether you are turning on the lights at home, working on a school computer, or running around your back yard, you are using energy. This chapter explores nonrenewable and renewable energy resources that we use every day. Coal, oil, and natural gas are examples of fossil fuels, which are nonrenewable energy. Fossil fuels take millions of years to form, so they cannot be replaced in your lifetime. The sun, wind, and water are renewable resources. This means they won't run out if we use them as energy.

FOSSIL FUELS

How many times have you turned on a light today? Have you ever wondered where that power comes from? Most of our electricity comes from burning fossil fuels. How did fossil fuels form?

Around 300 million years ago, the earth was hotter and wetter than it is today. Swamps with giant trees covered much of the earth's surface. When plants and animals died in these swamps, they were covered with layers of sand, clay, and minerals. Over millions of years, the pressure and heat from more and more layers turned the organic matter into fossil fuels.

COAL is found between layers of rock deep underground. It has been used as a fuel to melt copper and heat homes. In the 1800s, coal was burned to power steam engines in factories, trains, and ships. Today, coal produces about half of the electricity we use in America.

To get coal, people have to dig it up in mines. Children as young as 8 worked 18 hours a day in coal mines in England and America in the 1800s. Dangers included explosions and flooding tunnels. It wasn't until 1902 that the United States passed a law that children under 14 could not work in coal mines.

OIL has been used by people for 6,000 years. The ancient Egyptians treated cuts with oil and Native Americans made mosquito repellent out of it. They found oil above ground in seeps. This is an area where oil leaks up from below the earth's surface. They also skimmed it off lakes and streams.

Today, oil companies drill through rock to extract oil. It is pumped to the surface and then moved by pipeline or ship to where it is needed. Chemicals that come from oil are called petrochemicals. They are used to make lots of things you probably have in your house, such as plastic and laundry detergent.

THE CLIMATE IS CHANGING

The earth's atmosphere holds in some of the sun's energy and keeps the earth warm. Carbon dioxide is a greenhouse gas that also keeps the earth's surface warm. When we burn fossil fuels, it releases lots of greenhouse gases that get trapped by the earth's atmosphere. The trapped energy makes the earth's temperature rise in a process called **global warming**.

WORDS TO KNOW

global warming: an increase in the earth's average temperatures, enough to cause climate change.

THEN & NOW

In recent decades, yard clippings, food waste, and manure have been thought of as garbage.

Material from living or recently living organisms is called biomass. Today, people are discovering that biomass can be recycled and used to produce electricity, heat, and fuel.

Even an increase of 1 degree Fahrenheit can melt ice caps and glaciers. In 1850, Montana's Glacier National Park had 150 glaciers. Today, the park has only 25 glaciers! This has been caused by **climate change**.

RENEWABLE ENERGY RESOURCES

WORDS TO KNOW

climate change: changes to the average weather patterns in an area over a long period of time.

engineer: someone who uses science and math to build things.

Some experts believe that if we keep using fossil fuels, we'll use them all up. Oil could run out in 50 years, natural gas in 70 years, and coal in 250 years. Scientists and **engineers** are working to convert renewable resources, such as the sun and the wind, into energy.

SOLAR POWER comes from the sun, 93 million miles away from the earth. The sun is our most important source of energy. It only takes eight seconds for the sun's light to reach us. Without the sun, there would be no life on earth.

The sun is a mass of swirling gases—75 percent hydrogen and 25 percent helium. When these gases come together they create heat and light.

People can capture the sun's energy with **thermal systems** and **solar cells**. Some thermal systems use giant mirrors and **lenses** to store the sun's energy. It is later used for heat or electricity. Back in the 1400s, Leonardo da Vinci suggested that a mirror could be used to focus the sun's rays to heat water.

JUST FOR LAUGHS

WHY DID THE SUN GET GOOD GRADES AT SCHOOL?

Because it was bright!

Solar cells are different from thermal systems because they convert the sun's energy directly into electricity. Do you have a solar cell–powered calculator? Solar cells can power very small items such as calculators, but they can also supply electricity for large projects.

A massive, 50,000-seat stadium in Taiwan uses 8,844 solar panels to produce all of its electricity.

WORDS TO KNOW

thermal system: a way to store the sun's energy to generate heat.

solar cells: a device that converts the energy of the sun directly into electricity.

lens: a curved piece of glass that focuses light passing though it.

WHO WAS JOHN MUIR?

John Muir was a writer and a naturalist known as the "Father of the National Parks." He helped create America's first national park, Yosemite.

WIND ENERGY has been used for thousands of years to pump water and to sail ships. Today, people use **turbines** to capture the wind's energy. When the wind blows, blades spin a shaft connected to a **generator** that turns the energy into electricity. A large wind turbine can power 300 homes.

Many turbines grouped together are called a wind farm. One of the largest wind farms in the world is in Roscoe, Texas. The farm is several times the size of Manhattan in New York City. Its 627 turbines produce enough power for 250,000 homes!

WORDS TO KNOW

turbine: a machine with blades turned by the force of water, air, or steam.

generator: a machine that converts energy into electricity.

tidal: having to do with the daily rise and fall of ocean water.

DID YOU KNOW?

Do you like to play in ocean waves? They're a source of power that will never run out. Wave-powered plants harness **tidal** energy. In the Bay of Fundy in Canada, a tidal power system will use underwater turbines to provide power to 100,000 homes.

HYDROELECTRIC POWER comes from moving water. In a hydroelectric power plant, a turbine converts the power of moving water to electricity. California, Oregon, and Washington are home to the biggest hydroelectric plants in the United States.

While hydroelectric power is renewable, it does have disadvantages. Dams built to control the water damages surrounding ecosystems.

One of the largest dam projects in the world is the Three Gorges Dam in China. It produces eight times more electricity than the Hoover Dam in Colorado. To build the dam, the Chinese moved more than 1.2 million people. The dam has damaged habitat and **endangered** species such as the finless porpoise.

WORDS TO KNOW

endangered: putting a plant or animal species in danger of going extinct.

PEDAL POWER

Guests at a hotel in Copenhagen, Denmark, can help generate electricity by pedaling bicycles attached to the hotel's main power grid. The hotel's goal is to inspire guests to exercise and help the environment at the same time.

GEOTHERMAL

The closer you travel to the center of earth, the hotter it is. **Geothermal** energy comes from beneath the surface of the earth. The crust is the outer layer of the earth, nearest the surface. Beneath the crust is the mantle, with melted rock called **magma**.

Sometimes, geothermal energy escapes from beneath the surface of the earth. When a volcano erupts, large amounts of magma can flow out. Have you ever been to a **hot spring**? This is a place where hot water comes to the surface through cracks in rocks. When water explodes through these cracks, it is called a **geyser**. Old Faithful, in Yellowstone National Park, is the most famous geyser in America.

WORDS TO KNOW

geothermal: a renewable heat energy that comes from beneath the surface of the earth.

magma: hot, partially melted rock below the surface of the earth.

hot spring: a natural pool of water that is heated by hot or molten rock. Hot springs are found in areas with active volcanoes.

geyser: a jet of hot water.

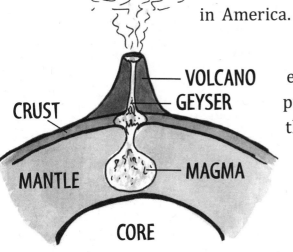

CRUST
VOLCANO
GEYSER
MANTLE
MAGMA
CORE

In some countries, geothermal energy is used to heat buildings and produce electricity. Iceland has more than 25 active volcanoes and many geysers. Geothermal energy heats 88 percent of all Icelandic homes.

BUILD A MINI TURBINE

A spinning turbine can be used to generate electricity. How can you get a turbine to spin?

1 Push a skewer into each end of the cork.

2 Cut six wide strips of plastic the length of the cork. Fold them in half lengthwise to make long flaps and glue them, evenly spaced, to the cork.

3 Attach your turbine by making holes at the ends of the container and inserting the skewers one at a time.

THINGS TO THINK ABOUT: What happens when you pour water over your turbine? Does more or less water make a difference? What happens if you attach something to one of the skewers sticking out of the plastic container?

SUPPLIES

- 2 wood skewers
- cork
- plastic file folder
- scissors
- waterproof glue
- plastic container
- water

REDUCING ENERGY USE

Most of the energy we use comes from nonrenewable resources that can't be replaced. Here are some ways to reduce your energy use.

* Use less electricity by turning off the lights when you leave a room or deciding what you want before opening the refrigerator.

* Hang your clothes to dry rather than drying them in a dryer.

* For errands close to home, walk or ride your bike.

* Instead of turning up the heat, put on a sweater.

* Instead of using an air conditioner, open a window or use a fan.

IT'S ACTIVITY TIME!

SOLAR MIRROR EXPERIMENT

Based on Leonardo da Vinci's solar mirror sketch, this experiment shows how the sun's energy can be used.

1 Start a scientific method worksheet. What is your hypothesis? Will the mirror increase the amount of energy collected from the sun? Why or why not?

2 Cut three pieces of black paper wide enough to cover the jars. Black paper absorbs the most sunlight.

3 Wrap the paper around the jars and secure each with a rubber band.

4 Place one jar in the shade and two jars in direct sunlight.

5 Position a mirror so that it directs sunlight onto one of the jars. Check the mirror every 30 minutes as the sun's position changes.

6 Take the temperature of each jar after 30 minutes and again after one hour. Write down your results. Is one jar warmer than the others? Graph your results.

THINGS TO THINK ABOUT: Do you think your results would differ if you didn't wrap the jars in black paper? Why or why not?

SUPPLIES

- science notebook
- pencil
- 3 empty glass jars
- black paper
- scissors
- 3 rubber bands
- makeup mirror
- thermometer

DESIGN A WIND-POWERED CAR

Every year, more environmentally friendly cars are being designed. Now it's your turn to create a wind-powered green energy car!

1 Using a ruler, pencil, and scissors, measure and cut the file folder into a rectangle, 4 by 6 inches (10 by 15 centimeters). This is the body of your car.

2 Tape a straw across each end of your car's body. Push a candy onto each of the four ends of the straws for wheels. Tape the ends so that your wheels do not come off, but make certain the wheels still move freely.

3 How can you create a wind catcher using scrap paper, fabric, paper cups, and egg cartons? Give some thought to your design, then build your wind catcher and attach it to your car.

4 Plug in an electric fan and place your car in front of the fan. Before you turn on the fan, draw a finish line.

5 Turn on the fan and use a stopwatch to time how long it takes your car to cross the finish line.

6 Modify your wind catcher and repeat this activity many times to find the best design.

THINGS TO TRY: Do you have a better idea for wheels? Try using a heavier base or adding weight to your car's body. How does this change the speed of your car?

SUPPLIES

- ruler and pencil
- scissors
- file folder
- tape and glue
- 4 to 6 plastic drinking straws
- 4 round candies with holes in them for the wheels
- scrap paper
- fabric scraps
- paper cups
- egg cartons
- electric fan
- stopwatch

CREATE A SOLAR OVEN

Have you ever tried cooking using the sun and a paper box? In this activity, you are going to make an oven that uses energy from the sun to cook food.

1 On the lid of your pizza box draw a rectangle roughly 8 by 5 inches (20 by 13 centimeters).

2 Carefully cut out three sides of the rectangle. Leave one side uncut to create a flap and a window.

3 Cover the inside of the rectangle with foil. Bend the foil over the top or glue it down to keep it in place.

4 Cover the window of the box with plastic wrap. Use clear tape to keep the plastic wrap in place.

5 Place the graham crackers, marshmallows, and chocolate on the tin pie plate. You're ready to cook a s'more. Open the pizza box and place the plate in the middle of your solar oven.

6 Position the solar oven on a flat surface in direct sunlight. Angle the foil lid to direct the sun onto your s'more. Tape a straw to hold the lid of the oven open.

7 Once your s'more has melted, enjoy!

THINGS TO TRY: Line the inside of the box with black paper. Try sealing any cracks along the sides of the box. What else can you do to help your oven keep in its heat?

SUPPLIES

- pizza box
- pencil
- scissors
- ruler
- tin foil
- glue
- plastic wrap
- clear tape
- 2 graham crackers
- 2 marshmallows
- chocolate
- tin pie plate
- drinking straw

CONSERVING EARTH'S RESOURCES

Our planet is packed with natural resources. But as you have learned, not all natural resources can be replaced. Even renewable resources are threatened by pollution. What can be done about this? Scientists, engineers, and people just like you are taking action.

Scientists and engineers are designing ways to make products out of materials once considered waste. They're using renewable energy resources to create new, **earth-friendly** inventions. Even the small daily decisions you make can conserve natural resources. Recycling and turning off the water while you brush your teeth can have an impact!

WORDS TO KNOW

earth-friendly: refers to something that won't harm the environment.

SMART TRANSPORT

Have you heard about cars running on batteries? How about planes flying on solar power? These are real inventions that show just how exciting **green technology** is.

People can drive a car that runs on gas or electricity, or a hybrid car that uses both gas and electricity. The choice you make is important. Today, there are 800 million cars on the road worldwide. The International Energy Agency predicts that by 2035 there will be 1.7 billion cars. That's a lot of greenhouses gases heading for the atmosphere! And if all those cars use gas, that means a big increase in demand for nonrenewable resources.

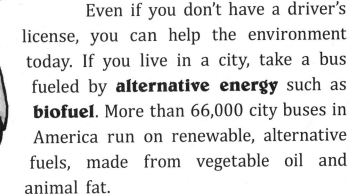

Even if you don't have a driver's license, you can help the environment today. If you live in a city, take a bus fueled by **alternative energy** such as **biofuel**. More than 66,000 city buses in America run on renewable, alternative fuels, made from vegetable oil and animal fat.

Taxis and planes are also going green. New York City introduced six electric cabs in 2013 to see if taxi drivers could find the time to charge their cabs for 60 to 90 minutes a day.

Soon, you'll be able to take an electric cab to an airport to meet a solar-powered plane. In 2013, a solar-powered plane called *Solar Impulse* successfully flew across the United States! It proved that it is possible to fly through the day and night without fossil fuels.

JUST FOR LAUGHS

HAVE YOU HEARD THE JOKE ABOUT THE DUMP?

Don't worry, it's a load of garbage!

WORDS TO KNOW

dependence: relying on someone or something.

Many of these projects have been designed to reduce our **dependence** on nonrenewable resources. They help people consider the solutions that can be created with renewable resources. If you were given a pile of trash, what would you build with it? Your creation could have a huge impact on the world!

WHO WAS RACHEL CARSON?

Rachel Carson was a scientist who wrote *Silent Spring* in 1962. The book made people think about how pollution affects the environment. Thanks to her book, scientists now know that certain chemicals are poisonous to soil, plants, and animals.

CHOICES

Governments are recognizing that many natural resources cannot be replaced. That's why governments are taking action and making laws that protect the air, water, and soil from pollution. These laws will protect natural resources and restore biodiversity.

Look around your town. People who care about the environment may be promoting lifestyles in your community that are earth-friendly. Advertisements can encourage people to save resources by changing their habits and behavior. Slogans such as "Do the earth a favor, be a power saver" send clear messages.

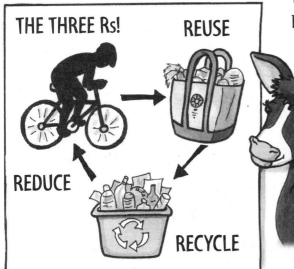

THE THREE Rs! REUSE REDUCE RECYCLE

WORDS TO KNOW

sustainable: when resources are used in a way that does not use them up.

waste management: the collecting, transporting, and disposing of waste.

Local farmers' markets sell food grown in a **sustainable** way. And better **waste management** systems give people more opportunities to practice the three Rs: reduce, reuse, and recycle.

RECYCLING

Much of our garbage ends up in landfills. You have probably tossed a soda can in the garbage. Did you know that your can will sit in a landfill for 100 years before breaking down? A plastic jug may take hundreds of years to break down. And a styrofoam cup might take millions of years. Nobody knows yet!

Think about how many natural resources it took to make those products. Now think about how many natural resources are being harmed when they are thrown away. Landfills are bad for soil, plants, and animals.

Your garbage doesn't have to sit in a landfill. You can recycle it. What exactly is recycling? When something new is made from something old, that's called recycling.

THREE ARROWS

In the 1970s, Gary Anderson created the recycling symbol for a contest in honor of the first Earth Day. The arrows represent reducing, reusing, and recycling. You'll find the logo everywhere, on paper and plastic packaging and metal cans.

BOTTLE BUILDING

The EcoArc Pavilion in Taiwan stands nine stories high and is made of 1.5 million plastic bottles. Water collected during rainstorms runs down the outside of the building and acts as an air conditioner.

Recycling is not a new idea. People have been recycling for thousands of years. The ancient Greeks melted down old weapons to create new ones, as did the Vikings. Recycling metal made sense because it was so difficult to extract it. Metal was a **scarce** resource.

WORDS TO KNOW

scarce: when there is very little of something.

In North American history, pioneers recycled and reused almost everything. Wagon boards became doors. Wooden barrels became chairs. Scrap fabric was turned into quilts. During WWII, scrap metal was collected for the war effort. Some people even collected foil gum wrappers!

Does your family take the recycling bin down to the curb each week? Curbside recycling did not start until the 1980s. Now more than 139 million people in America can place their recyclables by the curb. A typical bin includes newspapers, food jars, plastic containers, and cans. Once a truck collects the contents of your bin, it goes to a recycling plant, where it is sorted into paper, plastic, glass, and metal.

Paper is pressed flat and sold to a paper mill, where it is made into new products such as telephone directories or egg cartons. Plastic is cleaned, shredded, and cut into pellets.

The pellets might become a fleece top or a seat at a sports stadium. Glass is crushed and re-melted before being made into new jars. Metal is also melted down and made into new cans.

No matter what you choose to recycle, you are helping the environment. When you recycle, you are saving some new resources. Making an object from recycled materials uses less energy and cuts down on the amount of waste that ends up in landfills.

MORE RECYCLING IDEAS

There are more ways to recycle than just placing an object in a recycling bin. Cutting back on waste begins by buying less in the first place. This is called **source reduction**.

Ask yourself before you buy something if you really need it. If you do buy the product, choose one with little or no packaging— or packaging made from recycled material. A bar of soap has less packing than a soap pump. Frozen juice concentrate uses fewer resources than a jug of juice.

WORDS TO KNOW

source reduction: reducing waste by buying less.

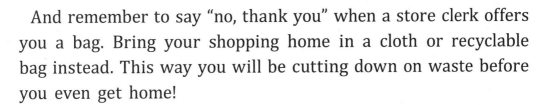

And remember to say "no, thank you" when a store clerk offers you a bag. Bring your shopping home in a cloth or recyclable bag instead. This way you will be cutting down on waste before you even get home!

Did you know the product you purchased may never need to be put in the recycling bin? Boxes and plastic containers can be used to make fun creations, like the ones in this book! Reusing containers is not just for kids either. Engineers in Seattle built a coffee shop with four shipping containers. And in a Paraguay village, people used materials found in a dump to create instruments for a children's orchestra!

YOU CAN DO IT!

Here are more ways you can help the environment and conserve natural resources. A few small changes can make a big difference.

* Trade toys you are no longer using with friends or donate old toys to charity.

* Repair broken objects.

* Take public transportation or carpool with friends.

* Eat your leftovers.

* Challenge yourself to a litter-free lunch. Use containers that can be washed and reused.

* Eat local food. This will cut down on the amount of carbon dioxide put into the atmosphere each year by vehicles bringing food from far away.

IT'S ACTIVITY TIME!

MAKE A REUSABLE T-SHIRT BAG

In an effort to reduce pollution, many towns and cities are banning plastic bags. You can make your own reusable and stylish bag from an old T-shirt. **CAUTION: Have an adult help with the iron.**

1 Cut the sleeves and neckband off the T-shirt.

2 Create a fun design on your T-shirt with crayons.

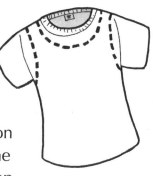

3 Ask an adult to heat-set the crayon design for you. Place the T-shirt on the ironing board with an old towel on top of it. With the iron on a low setting, press firmly down onto the T-shirt.

4 When the T-shirt has cooled, turn it inside out. Place a ruler along the bottom and draw a straight line across. This will be your stitch guide.

5 Make small stitches along the line to sew the seam and close the bottom of your bag. Turn the bag right side out and it is ready to use!

SUPPLIES

- scissors
- plain, old T-shirt
- crayons
- iron and ironing board
- old towel
- ruler
- pencil
- needle and thread

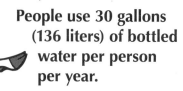

THEN & NOW

In 1976, Americans used 1.6 gallons (7 liters) of bottled water per person per year.

People use 30 gallons (136 liters) of bottled water per person per year.

MAKE YOUR OWN PAPER

Making paper out of paper scraps from your recycling bin is fun. **CAUTION: This activity uses hot water and a blender, so ask an adult for help.**

1 Tear up pieces of scrap paper or newsprint and place in a glass bowl. Pour hot water over the paper to soak for one hour.

2 Mix the soaked paper in the blender until it looks like oatmeal. Add a drop of food coloring, seeds, or leaves to give your paper pulp color and texture.

3 Place the screen into the tub and pour about 1 inch (3 centimeters) of water over it. Pour about 1 cup (240 milliliters) of the pulp onto the screen and spread it evenly.

4 Lift the screen up slowly and place it on one towel. Cover it with the other towel and use the rolling pin to press out the excess water.

5 Let the pulp dry overnight and carefully peel the paper off the screen.

THINGS TO TRY: Make paper out of grass clippings and leaves! You'll first need to soak the grass for at least an hour in a pot of water mixed with ½ cup (120 milliliters) of baking soda. Then, follow the steps as above. You can tell your friends your paper is made without chopping down trees.

SUPPLIES

- scrap paper or newsprint
- large glass bowl
- hot water
- blender
- food coloring
- seeds or leaves
- large flat tub at least 3 inches deep (8 centimeters)
- piece of window screen
- measuring cup
- 2 towels
- rolling pin

IT'S ACTIVITY TIME!

PLASTIC FANTASTIC CHALLENGE

Now that you have read about ways to reuse waste, here is your chance to design and build a structure out of materials found in your recycling bin.

1 Look through your recycling bin and sort the contents into plastic, paper, and metal.

2 On a piece of paper, sketch out your design for a building. During the design process, think about the following questions. How will your design be used? How will it retain heat or let it escape? How will it generate energy? How will it be lit?

3 Using tape, glue, or string, start building your design.

THINGS TO TRY: What else can you use in your design? Are there other ways to hold your structure together? Don't forget to decorate your building.

SUPPLIES

- ✪ contents of the recycling box, including plastic, paper, and metal
- ✪ paper
- ✪ pencil
- ✪ tape
- ✪ glue
- ✪ string

DID YOU KNOW?

In 2012, volunteers with International Coastal Cleanup collected 10 million pounds of marine trash, including plastic bags. The plastic bag industry says that plastic bags are not the problem—it is the people who do not dispose of them correctly.

GLOSSARY

Aboriginal: the first people who lived in Australia.

absorb: to soak up a liquid or take in energy, heat, light, or sound.

acid rain: precipitation that has been polluted by acid.

aerosol: ('air-oh-sul) a substance contained under pressure and released by a gas as a spray.

algae: ('al-gee) a simple organism found in water. It is like a plant but does not have roots, stems, or leaves.

alternative energy: energy generated in ways that do not use up natural resources or harm the environment.

anaerobic: (an-e-'roh-bik) living without oxygen.

atmosphere: ('at-muh-sfeer) the gases surrounding the earth or another planet.

BCE: put after a date, BCE stands for Before Common Era and counts years down to zero. CE stands for Common Era and counts years up from zero. The year this book was published is 2014 CE.

bedrock: the solid rock below the subsoil.

biodiversity: ('bih-oh-dev-'er-set-ee) the different plants, animals, and other living things in an area.

biofuel: fuel made from living matter, such as plants.

bond: a force that holds two things together.

carbon dioxide: ('kar-ben dy-ok-sihd) the gas that's produced as a waste product by your body.

chain reaction: when things are so connected that a change to one causes a change in the others.

climate change: changes to the average weather patterns in an area over a long period of time.

communication satellite: an object placed in orbit around the earth to relay television, radio, and telephone signals.

community: a group of people who live in the same area.

compost: to recycle food scraps and vegetation and put them back in the soil.

condense: when a vapor turns into a liquid.

conduct: to transfer something.

conserve: to avoid wasteful use of something.

contaminate: to pollute or make dirty.

crops: plants grown for food and other uses.

crust: the earth's outer layer.

crystal: a solid with its molecules arranged in a repeated pattern.

decay: to rot.

decomposers: organisms such as ants, worms, and fungi that break down wastes, dead plants, and dead animals. Fungi are organisms such as mold and mushrooms.

deforestation: when trees are cut down or burned to clear the land.

demand: how much of something people want.

dependence: relying on someone or something.

deposit: a layer of something, such as sand or salt.

desertification: when farmable land turns into desert.

displace: to force people or animals to move from their home.

drought: (drowt) a long period of time with little or no rain.

earth-friendly: refers to something that won't harm the environment.

ecosystem: ('ee-koh-sis-tem) a community of living and nonliving things and their environment. Living things are plants, animals, and insects. Nonliving things are soil, rocks, and water.

endangered: putting a plant or animal species in danger of going extinct.

energy: the ability to do work.

engineer: someone who uses science and math to build things.

GLOSSARY

environmentalist: (en-vy-ren-ment-el-est) a person who works to keep the earth healthy.

environment: everything in nature, living and nonliving, including animals, plants, rocks, soil, and water.

equator: (ee-'kway-ter) an invisible line circling the globe halfway between the North and South poles.

erosion: the gradual wearing away of rock or soil by water and wind.

evaporate: when a liquid turns into a vapor.

extinct: (ek-'stinkt) when a group of plants or animals dies out and there are no more left in the world.

extract: to remove or take out by effort or force.

factory: a place where goods are made.

fertile: good for growing crops.

fertilizer: any substance put on land to help crops grow better.

food chain: the feeding relationship between plants and animals in an environment.

fossil fuels: fuels made from the remains of ancient plants and animals, including coal, oil, petroleum, and natural gas.

fumes: gas, smoke, or vapor that is dangerous to inhale.

gas: a substance that can fill up a container, such as air filling your lungs. A gas does not have a definite shape—it spreads out to fill the space it's in.

generator: a machine that converts energy into electricity.

geothermal: (jee-oh-'ther-mel) a renewable heat energy that comes from beneath the surface of the earth.

geyser: ('gih-zer) a jet of hot water.

glacier: ('glay-sher) a large area of ice and snow.

global warming: an increase in the earth's average temperatures, enough to cause climate change.

goods: things to use or sell.

green technology: inventions that protect the environment or use renewable resources.

groundwater: water found in cracks or spaces beneath the surface of the earth.

habitat: an area that a plant or animal calls home.

hot spring: a natural pool of water that is heated by hot or molten rock. Hot springs are found in areas with active volcanoes.

humus: soil formed from decaying leaves and organisms.

Industrial Revolution: the name of the period of time that started in England in the late 1700s when people started using machines to make things in large factories.

industrial society: a society that relies on machines to make goods.

industry: the production of goods in factories.

iron: a strong, hard, magnetic metal.

landfill: a huge area of land where trash gets buried.

lens: a curved piece of glass that focuses light passing though it.

livestock: animals raised for food and other products.

magma: hot, partially melted rock below the surface of the earth.

manufacturing: to make large quantities of products in factories using machines.

marine: found in the ocean.

Middle East: the countries of Southwest Asia and North Africa, from Libya in the west to Afghanistan in the east.

mineral: something found in nature that is not an animal or plant, such as gold, salt, or copper.

molecule: ('mol-eh-kewl) the smallest amount of something.

natural resource: something from nature that people can use in some way, such as water, stone, and wood.

nonrenewable: something you can run out of, such as oil that will run out one day.

nutrients: substances in food and soil that living things need to live and grow.

orbit: the path of an object circling another object in space.

GLOSSARY

ore: a naturally occurring mineral that contains metal.

organic matter: decaying plants and animals that give soil its nutrients.

organism: ('or-gan-iz-em) any living thing.

overgraze: when animals eat all of the plants in an area.

ozone layer: the layer in the stratosphere that absorbs most of the sun's radiation.

pesticide: a chemical used to kill pests, such as insects.

petroleum: (pe-'troh-lee-em) a thick, dark liquid that occurs naturally beneath the surface of the earth. It can be separated into many products, including gasoline and other fuels.

photosynthesis: ('foh-toh-'sin-thes-es) the process a plant goes through to make its own food. The plant uses water and carbon dioxide in the presence of sunlight to make oxygen and sugar.

pollutant: something that makes the air, water, or soil dirty and damages the environment.

pollute: to make dirty or unclean with chemicals or other waste.

pore: a tiny opening.

power station: a place that generates electrical power.

precipitation: (pre-sip-it-'ay-shun) falling moisture in the form of rain, sleet, snow, and hail.

preserve: to keep safe from injury, harm, or destruction.

pressure: the force that pushes on any object.

raw material: a natural resource used to make something.

recycle: to use something again.

renewable: a resource that nature can replace.

reservoir: ('rez-e-vwar) a body of water that is stored for future use. It can be natural or man-made.

scarce: when there is very little of something.

sediment: bits of rock, sand, or dirt that have been carried to a place by water and wind.

sieve: (siv) a bowl or basket with lots of small holes in it.

slogan: a phrase used in advertising that is easy to remember.

smog: fog combined with smoke or other pollutants.

society: an organized community of people.

soil: the top layer of the earth, in which plants grow.

solar cells: a device that converts the energy of the sun directly into electricity.

source reduction: reducing waste by buying less.

species: ('spee-shees) a group of plants or animals that are related and look the same.

subsoil: the layer of soil beneath the topsoil.

sustainable: when resources are used in a way that does not use them up.

thermal system: a way to store the sun's energy to generate heat.

tidal: having to do with the daily rise and fall of ocean water.

topsoil: the upper layer of soil.

toxic: poisonous.

translucent: allowing some light to pass through.

turbine: a machine with blades turned by the force of water, air, or steam.

ultraviolet: invisible energy produced by the sun.

volatile organic compound (VOC): (vol-a-'tihl) a kind of chemical that can be harmful to humans and the environment.

waste management: the collecting, transporting, and disposing of waste.

waste: unwanted material that can harm the environment.

water cycle: the continuous movement of water from the earth to the clouds and back to earth again.

water treatment plant: a place where water is cleaned.

water vapor: water as a gas, such as steam, mist, or fog.

RESOURCES

BOOKS

Amsel, Sheri. *The Everything Kids Environment Book*. Adams Media, 2007.

Barraclough, Sue. *Earth's Resources*. Heinemann Raintree, 2008.

Burton, Bob. *Endangered Environments!* Gareth Stevens Publishing, 1996.

Cronin, Ali. *Making a Difference: The Changing the World Handbook*. Crabtree, 2009.

Davies, Nicola. *Extreme Animals: The Toughest Creatures on Earth*. Candlewick, 2006.

Javna, Sophie. *The New 50 Simple Things Kids Can Do To Save the Earth*. Andrews McMeel Publishing, 2009.

Kirk, Ellen. *Human Footprint*. National Geographic Children's Books, 2011.

Latham, Donna. *Amazing Biome Projects You Can Build Yourself*. Nomad Press, 2009.

Light Brown, Cynthia, and Brown, Nick. *Explore Rocks and Minerals!* Nomad Press, 2010.

McCarthy, Pat. *Friends of the Earth: A History of American Environmentalism*. Chicago Review Press, 2013.

Reilly, Kathleen. *Planet Earth: 25 Environmental Projects You Can Build Yourself*. Nomad Press, 2008.

Siddals, Mary McKenna. *Compost Stew*. Tricycle Press, 2010.

Thornhill, Jan. *This Is My Planet: The Kids' Guide to Global Warming*. Maple Tree Press, 2007.

VanCleave, Janice. *Science Around the World: Activities on Biomes From Pole to Pole*. Wiley, 2004.

Yasuda, Anita. *Explore Water!* Nomad Press, 2011.

WEB SITES

EPA Environmental Kids Club: *epa.gov/students*

National Geographic Kids: *kids.nationalgeographic.com/kids*

EcoKids: *ecokids.ca/pub/index.cfm*

Earth Matters 4 Kids: *earthmatters4kids.org/main.html*

Eco Friendly Kids: *ecofriendlykids.co.uk/naturalresourcesearth.html*

National Institute of Environmental Health Services: *kids.niehs.nih.gov/explore/reduce*

Science Kids: *sciencekids.co.nz/recycling.html*

Climate Kids: NASA's Eyes on the Earth: *climatekids.nasa.gov/recycle-this*

Kids Be Green: *kidsbegreen.org*

Time for Kids: Environment: *timeforkids.com/minisite/environment*

MUSEUMS

Museum of Science Boston: *mos.org*

American Museum of Natural History: *amnh.org*

Exploratorium: *exploratorium.edu*

Montshire Museum of Science: *montshire.org*

Museum of Science & History: *themosh.org/home.html*

North Carolina Museum of Natural Sciences: *naturalsciences.org*

The Houston Museum of Natural Science: *hmns.org*

California Science Center: *californiasciencecenter.org*

Museum of Science and Industry Chicago: *msichicago.org*

Pacific Science Center: *pacificsciencecenter.org*

Saint Louis Science Center: *slsc.org*

The Franklin Institute: *fi.edu*

Liberty Science Center: *lsc.org*

Fernbank Science Center: *fernbank.edu*

California Academy of Sciences: *calacademy.org*

INDEX